# FUN WITH THE DRUMS

by John Brophy

This book is not intended to be used as a method book — it's purpose is to be used as a supplemental text to help the student and keep his interest high while at the same time making it an educational situation! The student should pay close attention to the accents where indicated — they are there for definite reasons. On all exercises and solos it is important that the student practice slowly and thoroughly at first — then increase the speed. However, he should be constantly aware of accuracy even at faster tempos.

*John Brophy*

© 1973 BY MEL BAY PUBLICATIONS, INC.
ALL RIGHTS RESERVED. INTERNATIONAL COPYRIGHT SECURED. MADE AND PRINTED IN U.S.A.
No part of this publication may be reproduced in whole or in part, or stored in a retrieval system, or transmitted in any form
or by any means, electronic, mechanical, photocopy, recording, or otherwise, without written permission of the publisher.

**Visit us on the Web at www.melbay.com — E-mail us at email@melbay.com**

# Rudiments and Stickings
# Flams

### Single Flams

Played when one flam follows another, Flams alternate Left to Right.

### Flam taps-2

Flams—with a note in between. Flams alternate Left to Right.

### Flam and 2 taps-2

Flams—with 2 notes in between. Flams alternate Left to Right.

or

### Flam and 3 taps-2

Flams—with 3 notes in between. Flams do not alternate.

### Flam Parididdle-2

Flams—with the Parididdle Sticking. Flams alternate Left to Right.

© Copyright 1973 by Mel Bay Publications, Inc.,
International Copyright Secured, All Right Reserved,
Printed in U. S. A

 Single Parididdle

When one hand doubles, lift the opposite hand to prepare for the up-coming accented note.

 Double Parididdle

# Rolls

Stroke Motion

 5 Stroke

This Roll must be practiced alternating.

Stroke Motion

 7 Stroke

The Roll does not alternate but may be started on either hand.

Stroke Motion

 9 Stroke

This Roll alternates- it becomes an extension of the 5 stroke with two extra doubles on the beginning.

4

# Exercise in Quarter Notes

## The Student Must Count Aloud

These Exercises should be practiced

#1. Individual Line.

#2. As one entire exercise without stopping between lines.

#3. Then turn the book upside down and play both above again.

# Duet for 1 or 2 in Quarter Notes

This should be played as a duet or solo. Right Hand top line-Left Hand bottom line.

# Study in Quarter and Eighth Notes

Make sure to count aloud.

# Duet for 1 or 2 in Quarter and Eighth Notes

## Exercises for Eighth note Rests

# Duet 1 or 2 Eighth Rests

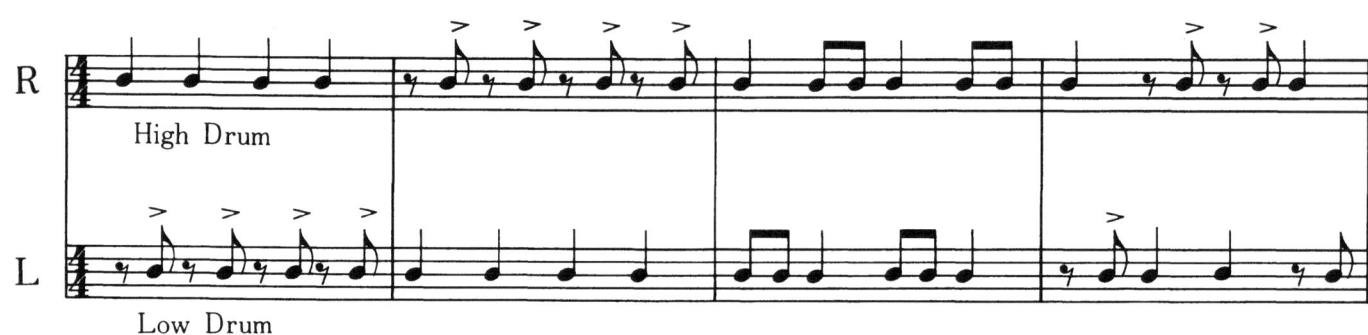

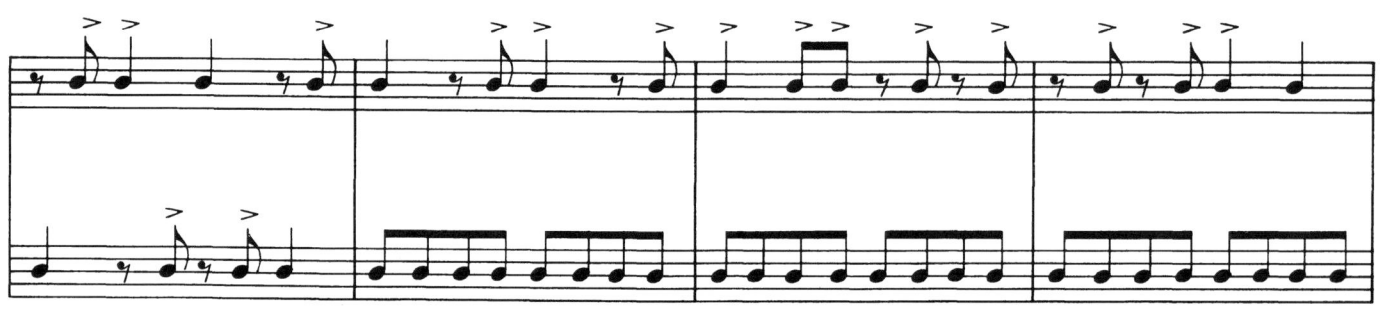

Play as Solo or Duet

# Eighth Note + Sixteenths Combination

## 1-and-ah Patterns

1&ah 2 & 3+4+etc.

## 1-e-and Patterns

1e+2+3+4+etc.

♫♪ and ♪♫ Keep the accent on the down beat part of the beat. I have found this effective in large passages of ♫♪. Often 8 beats usually begin to sound like ♩♫ and less like ♫♩

# Combination Patterns

Play as Solo and Duet

# Studies in Triplets

## Duet in Triplets

# Duet in Rhythm

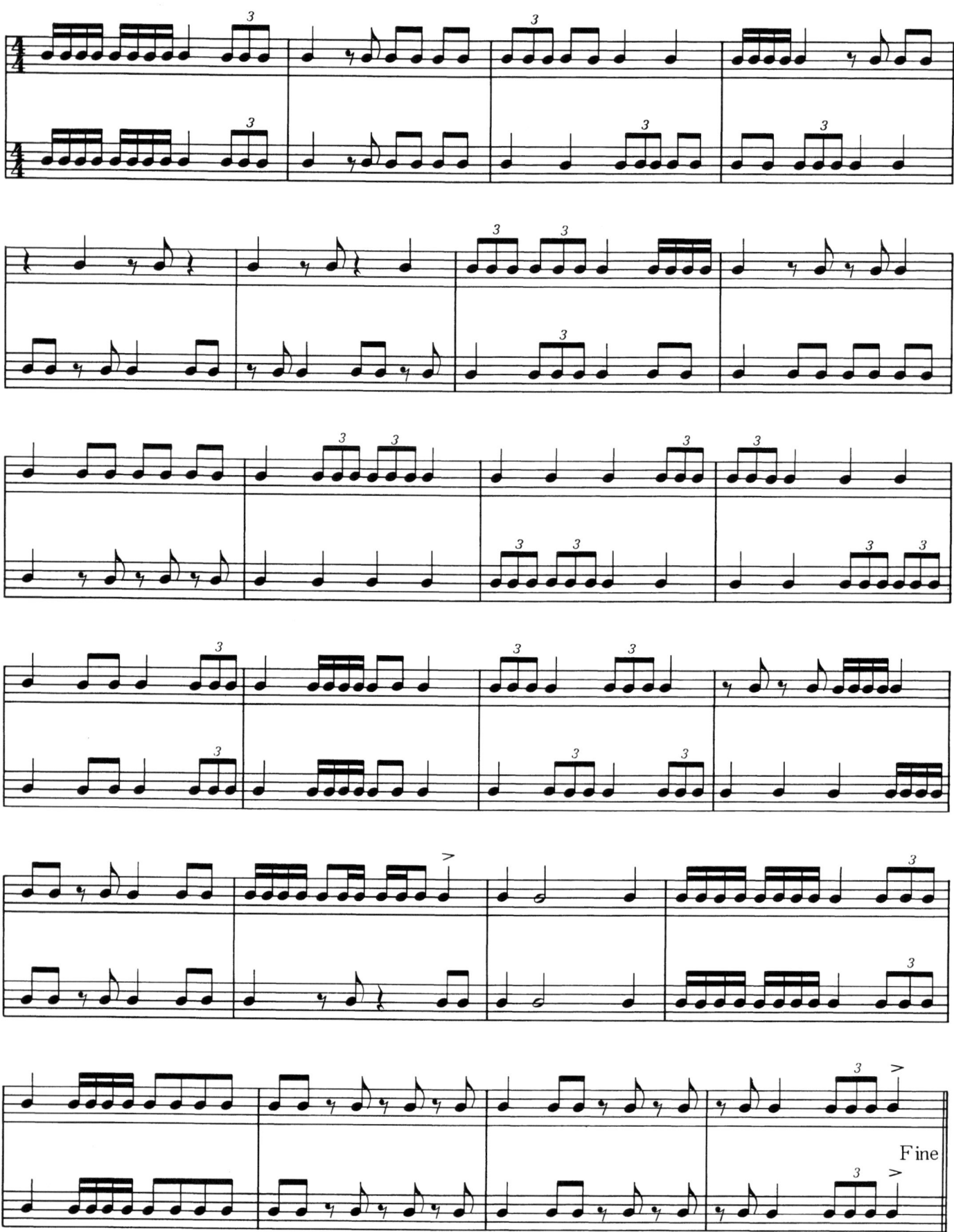

# Syncopation

# Solo #1 (without Flams)

# Fun With Flams

15

   Single Flams

One flam is followed by another unless enough rest is provided so the same flam may be repeated.

Example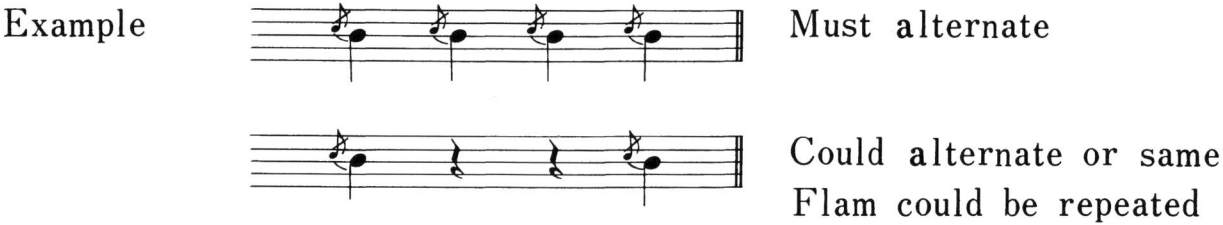

Must alternate

Could alternate or same Flam could be repeated

Make sure when you play the Flam you cannot distinguish between the tap and stroke— If you can hear a TA-DA separate sound, then you are playing them wrong.

## Motion is important in playing Flams

On a right flam the right stick is **7″** to **9″** off the drum—the left stick is **3″** to **4″** off the drum. After the flam is played, the position is immediately reversed. Left hand up and right hand down. Now the student is prepared to play the Left Flam.

This description holds true for all flam rudinents. The distance from the drum shortens as the speed of the flams increases. However the motion is still retained even when performing the flams rapidly.

**Picture shows position for a right flam.**

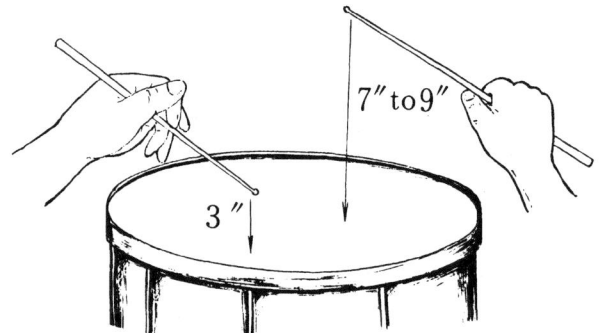

Many students have trouble playing flams because they do not realize flams do not change the rhythm of the music; they only enhance it.

Flam taps

On the flam tap the motion of the stick reverses on the tap Left stick comes up when the right tap is played — Right stick comes up when the left tap is played. Flam tap is played anytime a note comes between two Flams.

Other Examples:

All are flam taps.

Flam and 2 taps  Played anytime two notes come in between 2 Flams.

Other Examples:

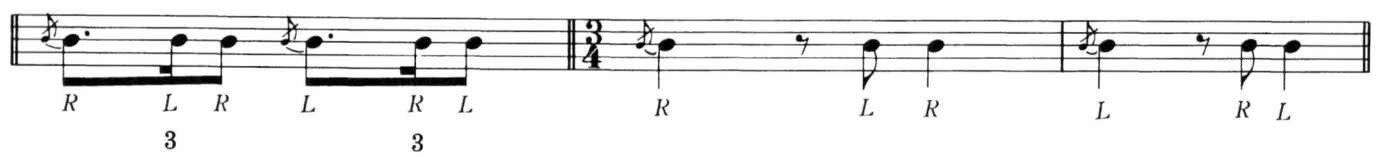

etc. - - - - - - -

# Solo #2 with Flams

Rehearse these lines slowly and carefully, first being careful of the sticking. Then practice the solo.

# Rolls

Long Roll

Indefinite (non—measured roll)

The student should approach the roll from two directions: fast bounces and controlled stroke taps.

 Slow to fast

Fast Bounces - the students should allow the right stick to bounce as many times as possible. When it is finished, then bounce the left. As speed increases, overlap the strokes, still allowing the stick to bounce as much as possible. — Do not restrict the bouncing of the stick; it will stop only when it is pulled off the head to overlap the opposite hand. As the speed increases the bounces will become fewer in each hand down to 3 in each hand and then finally 2 in each, producing a buzz type roll. Remember when using both these approaches, there is not an accent in the right or left hand. Keep the sound as even as possible. Left=Right Hand. Rolls like flams do not change the rhythms, they only enhance it or extend it.

Ex.

Same with Roll

There are many books on the use of the **5, 7, 9,** Stroke Rolls etc Generally, however, these rolls are used as follows:

# Solo for Two Drums 1 Player

# Flying High for four Drums

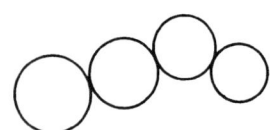

(2 Snares + Bongos)  (4 Snare Drums)  (1 Snare + 3 Toms)

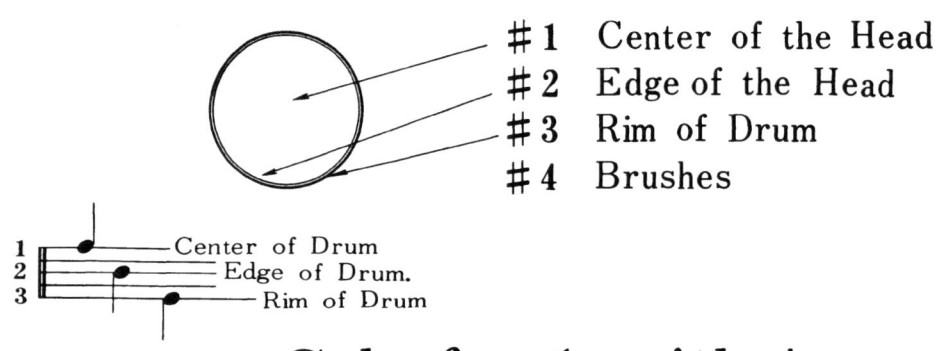

# Solo for 1 with 4

# Odd meters 5/4 7/4

## 5/4 Time Divided Either (3+2) or (2+3)

## Solo in 5/4 Time

5/8 or 5/16 Time signatures would be counted and/felt the same.

# $\frac{7}{4}$ Time

$\frac{7}{4}$ Time may be divided in many ways

# Solo in $\frac{7}{4}$

# Exercises in 3/4  3/8  6/8  9/8  12/8

All of following exercises are exactly the same except for the meter signature. The exercises should be used to show the student similarity among the various groupings of 3 pulses to a beat.

## #1 in 3/4

# #2 in 3/8

# Easy Dance Beats for Snare Drum

Right hand is used with a brush on the edge, with a stick on the edge, with the stick on the rim or with a suspended cymbal if available.

# Easy Drum Cadences

May be used with Snare and Bass Drum
Snare and Tenor Drum
Two Snare Drums

## 8 Count Cadences

Repeat as needed

## More Advanced Cadences

#1

# Parididdle Cadence

30

# 5

# 6

## Extended Cadence in 4/4

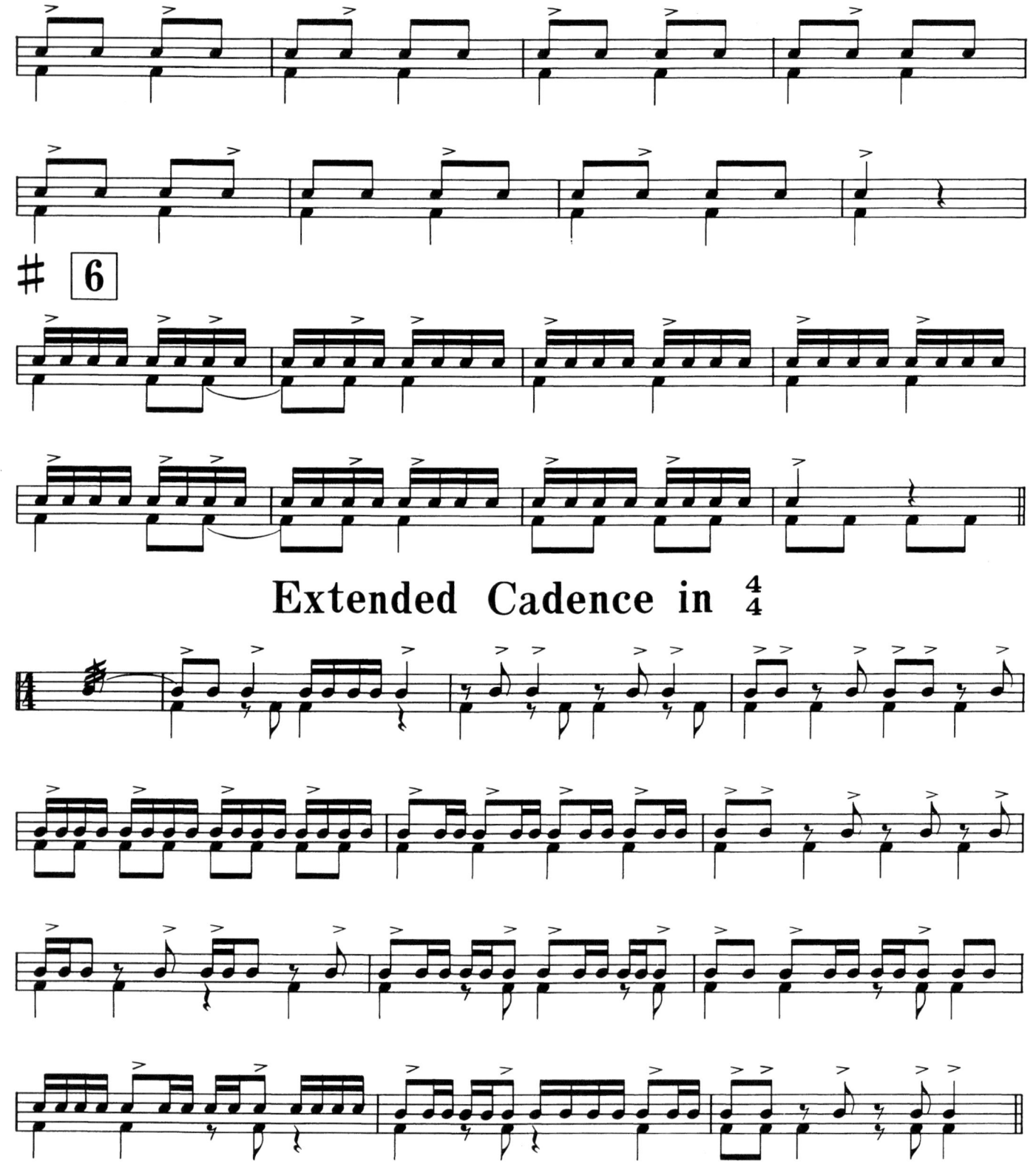

Try having your student memorize the above cadence.

# Easy Rock Beat for Bass Snare Hi-Hat and Ride Cymbal

## Hi-Hat is always played on beats 2 and 4

# Medium Rock Beats

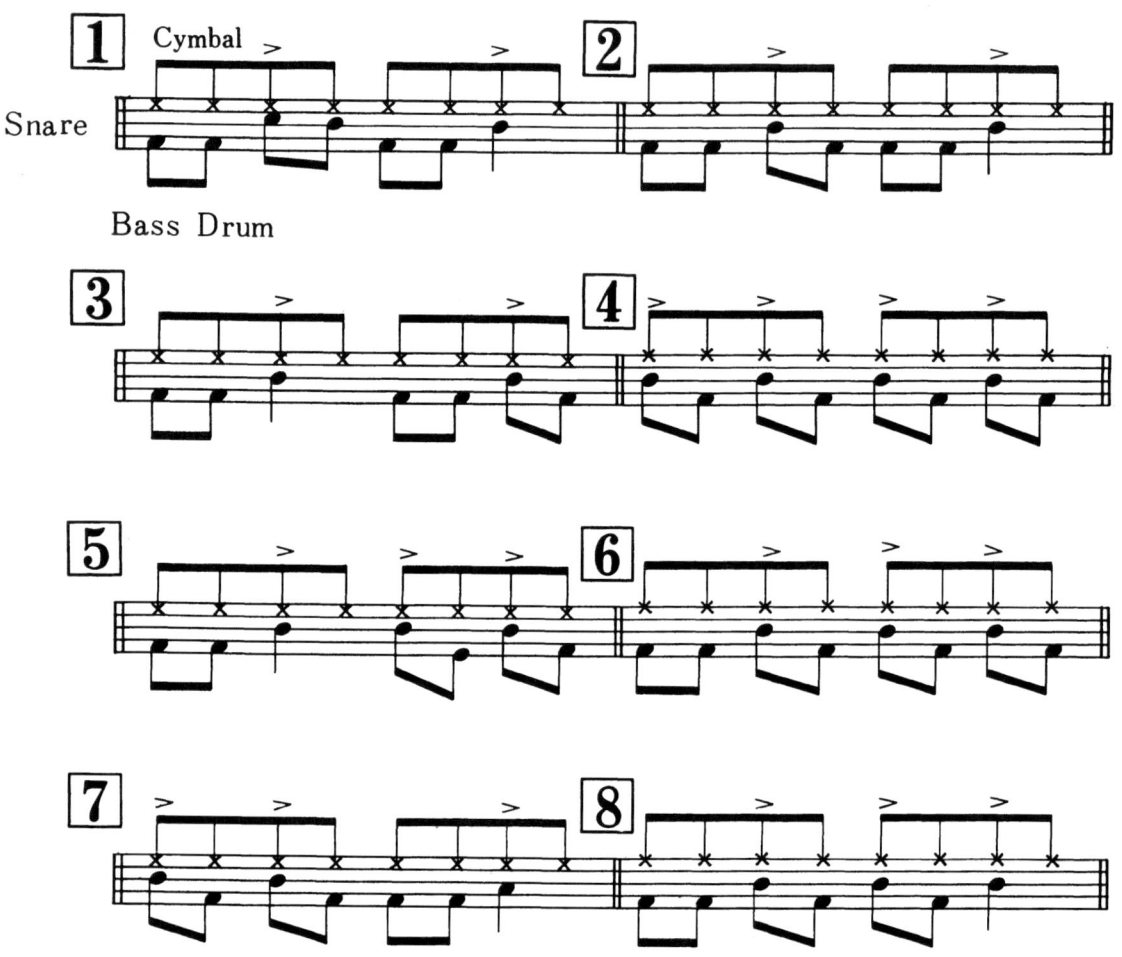

The above exercises should be done in combination.

Ex.

Also, they should be practiced with

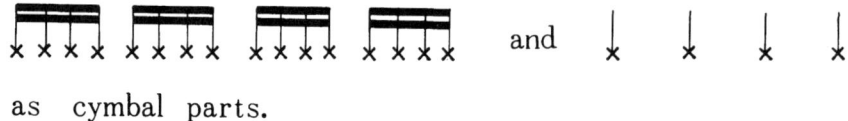

as cymbal parts.